ZamZam's
Faith in the Middle

Luella Faith Holwerda

AuthorHouse™
1663 Liberty Drive
Bloomington, IN 47403
www.authorhouse.com
Phone: 1-800-839-8640

First published by AuthorHouse   03/15/2011

ISBN: 978-1-4567-3039-0 (sc)

Library of Congress Control Number: 2011901420

Printed in the United States of America

Any people depicted in stock imagery provided by Thinkstock are models, and such images are being used for illustrative purposes only.
Certain stock imagery © Thinkstock.

This book is printed on acid-free paper.

Because of the dynamic nature of the Internet, any web addresses or links contained in this book may have changed since publication and may no longer be valid. The views expressed in this work are solely those of the author and do not necessarily reflect the views of the publisher, and the publisher hereby disclaims any responsibility for them.

authorHOUSE®

Dedicated

In memory of my wonderful Mother and Dad who gave me a rich legacy of faith and love.

To my patient, encouraging, and supportive husband Jim. I couldn't have written this without him! He has been my constant cheerleader and editor-in-progress, surprising me with comments and suggestions--not only to the manuscript, but also to my thoughts and ideas before they were even written on paper.

And to Mary, Steven, Kisky, Gunnar, Sina, Davis, Ellie, and Tessa, our precious grandchildren, who have been the true inspiration and motivation for the writing of this book for children.

Acknowledgements:

So many people have been involved in getting "Faith in the Middle" published for children, and I want to acknowledge and thank them:

My Mother's memoirs, Eleanor's "Miracle at Sea", and hours and hours of sharing emotions and memories with my brothers and sisters through the years have all been instrumental in triggering my memory, adding details to what I couldn't remember, and ultimately moving me to write. Thank-you, Laurence, Eleanor, Evelyn, Wilfred, and Lois!

The children in my classes at Central Elementary School in Brookings, South Dakota, who first showed me how meaningful and powerful the ZAMZAM story is for children. Thank-you, kids, for the great memories with you!

My niece, Jeni Paltiel, who years ago communicated the phrase "Right in the middle of America" to me, and now I used it to develop the repetitious "right in the middle" theme. Thank-you so much, Jeni!

Our youngest granddaughter, Tessa, who at age 10 was the perfect age to serve as the one and only children's editor. Thank-you, dear Tessa!

An additional thank-you goes to Sister Lois who wrote my bio on the back cover, generously enhancing and glorifying my talents so that I hardly recognized myself.

The attendees at the ZAMZAM Reunion in July, 2010 in Lancaster, Pennsylvania, who were relentless in encouraging me to publish for children. You made the difference. Thank-you for your confidence!.

Our own children, Terri, Steve, and Kristin, who have so many times witnessed first-hand the emotion their Mom has when telling the ZAMZAM story, and have patiently listened and embraced it. Thank-you!

And to God who has never left me.

My name is Luella Faith, and a long time ago, I was a little girl. I lived with my family in Kansas, right in the middle of America.

I liked my name a bunch. It sounded kind of pretty, it wasn't extra long, and I didn't know anyone else who had the same name. Mama and Daddy never told me where they got my first name, but they told me where they got "Faith". They chose it because they had so much faith in God. Perhaps another good name for me, though, would have been "Luella Right-in-the-Middle," because that's where I always was---- right in the middle of my family, who lived right in the middle of a little town, right in the middle of Kansas, right in the middle of America.

It was good to be right in the middle. That meant there were big kids to help me, and little kids to play with. Laurence was a big kid, my big brother. He was fun and strong and the best big brother anyone could have. We treated him like a king. Eleanor was the next big kid. She was my sister and she could bake bread and do the ironing when she was only eight years old. That was amazing! Then there was one more big kid and that was Evelyn. She was perfect because she didn't like to argue and she always shared her toys and treats with me. I loved that!

| Laurence | Eleanor | Evelyn | Me--Luella | Wilfred | Lois |
| Ray | Grace | Ruth | Faith | David | Christine |

Next it was me—Luella Right-in-the-Middle. My feelings were hurt easily, so I tried to never hurt anyone else's feelings. I also tried to be a good big sister to Wilfred. He was really cute and nice, so we would hold hands and do lots of things together. Sometimes we played house with Lois, and that was always fun. She was our baby sister and she had the biggest brown eyes that sparkled and made everybody smile. If you are counting, you now know that our family had six kids.

Daddy   Mama

I want to tell you about Mama and Daddy too. Mama was so beautiful and I loved to sit and brush her dark brown hair. Daddy was patient and smart and helpful. Together they were missionaries who went to Africa to tell the people about God. Sometimes I thought Daddy seemed like God himself because he never did anything bad. Besides, he preached very long sermons and prayed very long prayers. He was important to the African people. Mama was important too, but she didn't preach. Instead she listened and was kind and gentle. When she talked about someone, she only said nice things. I wish everyone could have a sweet Mama like I had and a Daddy who was a little bit like God.

Everyone thought we lived in an ordinary house, but I didn't think it was ordinary at all! I thought it was special. We had room for all of us even though there were only three bedrooms and one bathroom. We just cooperated a lot and had so much fun. Sometimes my sisters and I would hop into one bed together to talk and giggle. That is when I wanted to be right in the middle.

Our house was also a happy house. We laughed and played games every day. Hide-and-go-seek was the best because there were five big closets to hide in, and if you hid right in the middle, you would be found right away. But if you snuck way back into a dark corner and stayed very quiet, no one could find you for a long time. That's where I always tried to hide.

Down in our basement was a ping-pong table. It sat right in the middle so we could roller skate around and around it. Outside was a big yard with a sandbox and a swing hanging from a pear tree. There also was a barn in our yard, and in it we kept chickens and goats. One time it was so hot in the barn, that Mama brought all of her new, tiny, yellow, soft baby chicks right into the middle of our kitchen! Can you believe that? There was always a lot going on in our house right in the middle of town, in the middle of Kansas, in the middle of America—and right in the middle of our kitchen!

When I was three years old, my family sat down in the middle of our living room. The Africans had sent a letter saying they wanted Daddy to come back and tell them more about God. They also wanted him to help build more hospitals, churches, and schools. Daddy read the letter to us very carefully, and we talked about it. He understood how much the Africans needed him. He wanted to go and help. Mama wanted to go too. We all wanted to go! It would be like going back home. (Do you know I was born in Africa, just in a little house—not even in a hospital, but there was a missionary doctor and nurse who helped me get born?)

Going to Africa was a big problem, though, because there was a war going on. Some countries were fighting each other with bombs and guns and airplanes and submarines and warships. That made a lot of danger.

Another problem was that there is a big ocean between America and Africa. The only way to get across the ocean would be by either a boat or an airplane. Long ago when I was little, only movie stars and presidents flew in airplanes. Ordinary people like our family went by boat. A warship or airplane might attack us if we were on a boat in the middle of the ocean. We didn't know what to do.

We talked and then we prayed. God could help us make a decision, and He did! We decided that Daddy would go to Africa by himself because there was a lot of work for him to do. Mama would stay with us kids in our little town in the middle of Kansas, but when it was safe to travel, she would take us all to Africa to live with Daddy.

Daddy left for Africa on a hot day right in the middle of summer and it was very, very sad. I cried. Even big Laurence cried, but little Wilfred cried the most. He held onto Daddy and would not let go! He held so tight that Mama had to take him and hug and hold him while Daddy walked away with his head hanging down.

Three weeks after Daddy left, I had my birthday. Mama baked a cake and I felt so big when she put four candles right in the middle and lit them. I looked at those four shining candles and thought about the best wish in the world. Then I blew them out!

Do you know what my wish was? I wished that when I turned five, our family would all be together in the middle of Africa!

Days went by. Weeks went by. Months went by. Daddy was in Africa and Mama was with us kids in our house with the five closets in Kansas. We went Trick or Treating on Halloween. We had Thanksgiving turkey. We put up our Christmas tree. Then it was Valentines Day. I was tired of waiting. We were all tired of waiting! March came, and at last it looked like my birthday wish would come true. A ship named ZAMZAM was going to Africa, and it had room on it for us. There was a safe way for us to go to live with Daddy!!

Eleanor, Evelyn and I made up songs about the ZAMZAM, and we danced around the house singing, "ZAMZAM! ZAMZAM!" Wilfred and Lois danced and sang with us too, but Laurence thought we were kind of silly. We were going to Africa!

Mama didn't have time to dance. There were only ten days for her to get everything ready. She had to work fast. There were no big stores in Africa, so Mama had to go shopping. She bought underwear, socks, shoes, thread, material, books, crayons, and other stuff like that. Next she started packing. She had boxes right in the middle of every room in our house. She stuffed each one full. And right in the middle of all the packing, she took us to the doctor to get shots. Those shots hurt a lot, but we didn't want to get sick in Africa!

On the last night, Mama didn't go to bed for even one minute. She stayed up all night, and in the morning everything was packed. We were ready to go to Africa and the ZAMZAM was waiting for us in New York.

It was a long way from Kansas to New York. For two days we rode on the train. People looked at us and were surprised to see six children traveling with just one mama. But our Mama knew just how to take care of us. She said we should be quiet and not bother anyone, but she also showed us a big bag of treats. I was very quiet and good, and I ate a lot of treats.

New York was big and noisy with so many cars and people! It wasn't at all like Kansas! There were tall buildings that touched the clouds, and right next to these buildings was the ocean, and right there floating on the ocean was our ZAMZAM. It looked strong and safe with a big smokestack right in the middle. A gangplank made a bridge from the land to the ZAMZAM. We walked over the gangplank and onto the deck of our big boat.

Mama found the two rooms for our family right in the middle of the ship. There were bunk beds for us, and a sink, but no toilet. We had to go out on the deck to another door to find the bathroom. Mama had brought a baby buggy for little Lois to sleep in. Everything was perfect! Pretty soon we would see our Daddy!

The ZAMZAM was full of people! Some were missionaries with little kids like us. Some were big men who drove ambulances or teachers who wanted to have school every day. There also were nurses and doctors, cooks, newspaper writers, and the captain with his sailors and crew. We were more than three hundred people on the ZAMZAM and our ship was going to Africa!

I loved being on the ship. It was fun. The big kids had school while Wilfred, Lois, and I played together and tried to be good for Mama. Since I was a big sister to them, I helped keep Wilfred and Lois right in the middle of the deck so that they wouldn't fall over the edge into the ocean.

One day there was a lifeboat drill. We practiced putting on our lifejackets and going to our lifeboat station. That's when Mama discovered that we only had six lifejackets for our family. There was no little lifejacket for Lois. Mama knew that everyone should have a lifejacket—even if they were only one year old! She marched to the ship's office and asked for another lifejacket.

At first no one was going to help her. The man in the office said a one-year-old baby did not need a lifejacket because she would drown anyway! Mama would not listen to that. She sat down on the bench right in the middle of that office and said she would not leave until they gave her a lifejacket for her baby.

After awhile, they gave her one more jacket. It was too big for Lois, and it had holes in it, but Mama said thank-you. She was happy because she knew she could fix it. She made that jacket smaller and mended all of the holes. Then she mended all of our lifejackets. Mama could do anything. She was like Superman—really Superwoman!

During the next days, we prayed extra prayers. The captain told us he had seen some warships which may attack our ZAMZAM. We weren't safe after all!

1941	APRIL					1941
Sunday	Monday	Tuesday	Wednesday	Thursday	Friday	Saturday
		1	2	3	4	5
6	7	8	9	10	11	12
13	14	15	16	17	18	19
20 /27	21 /28	22 /29	23 /30	24	25	26

Then it happened!!! I didn't know how to read a calendar, but the date was April 17th. The year was 1941, and it was very early in the morning before we could see the sun shining. I was 4 years old—really 4 and 1/2. Laurence was 10, Eleanor was 8, Evelyn was 7, Wilfred was 3, and Lois was 1. Mama was 41. We were sound asleep right in the middle of our rooms. CRASH! BOOM! A loud explosion shook our beds! It was louder than thunder! Our sink crashed to the floor and the mirror fell off the wall and broke into hundreds of pieces. Mama told us to be careful, but she stepped right on some glass. Her foot started bleeding really bad and she didn't have time to take care of it.

And then CRASH! BANG! BOOM! The explosions and shaking happened all over again. And again! The floor tipped more and more to one side. We could hardly stand up. Wilfred, Lois, and I cried, but Mama was very calm. She didn't know what was happening, but she told us to put on our lifejackets and to be brave in Jesus. The ZAMZAM kept exploding! We could hear more shells coming, and sometimes they would miss us. And then another one would hit us! It smelled like firecrackers. It was a bad, bad morning!

A man with blood running down his face came to our door. He told us that a warship was firing big shells at us and wanted to sink us to the bottom of the ocean. Our ZAMZAM was right in the middle of a war!!!

Now we had to remember everything we had practiced in our lifeboat drill like tying our lifejackets tight and going as fast as we could to our lifeboat station. Laurence, Eleanor, and Evelyn were big helpers, but I couldn't tie my own lifejacket. Wilfred and Lois couldn't do it either. We needed a lot of help and we were scared. Mama and our big brother and sisters helped us. They got us ready. That was when Mama was the most brave of all. She just looked at us with lots of love and prayed out-loud, "Lord, save us. And take care of our Daddy if this is our last morning."

Mama picked up Lois and knew that Wilfred needed to be carried too, but her arms were already full. I got as close to Mama as I could and held onto her skirt real tight. I wished someone could carry me. Out the door we went, holding onto each other. My lifejacket puffed out like a dirty pillow under my chin and I did not like it. I didn't like anything about this morning. I heard screaming and crying. I saw the blood dripping from Mama's foot. I saw Mama limp and I held onto her skirt even tighter. We all stayed as close to each other as we could. This was a bad morning!

It wasn't light yet, but we found our lifeboat. Someone lifted me in. Our family snuggled together right in the middle. Other people were in our boat too. Then it was lowered over the side of the ZAMZAM toward the water. The only good thing was that all seven of us were together, but I sure wished our Daddy were there to help. We needed him and he could hold me!

Our lifeboat touched the water. We were in the middle of the ocean and there was no land anywhere. Every place I looked, all I saw was water and then more water. It didn't seem very safe to me! The ZAMZAM had a big hole in it and was tipping over to one side right next to us. I was afraid it would fall over on top of me. Mama kept saying again and again, "Little kiddies, be brave in Jesus. He loves you like Mama and Daddy do." I tried to be very brave, but it was hard to be big and brave when you are so little in the middle of a big ocean, and no one can hold you!

Oh no! My feet started to get wet! Wilfred's feet got wet! Laurence, Eleanor, and Evelyn's feet got wet. Everybody's feet got wet except for little Lois', and that was because Mama was holding her. There was water in the bottom of our lifeboat and it was getting deeper and deeper and deeper. We had to get the water out!

Some of the men dipped out water with their caps and shoes, but they couldn't dip fast enough. They tried to go faster and faster, but nothing helped. There were holes from the shells in the bottom of our lifeboat and it was leaking fast! We yelled for help, but there was no one to help us. Our lifeboat was so full of water, it couldn't float any longer! I was sitting in water all the way up past my tummy. I stretched as high as I could so no water would splash on my face.

"Laurence, watch out for Luella. Eleanor and Evelyn, stay close together. Wilfred, stay close to Mama. Lois, I will hold you tight. Children, be brave in Jesus. Remember He loves you and so do Mama and Daddy." These were the words I heard my brave Mama say. She talked very quietly and then.........................

Down we went! Our lifeboat sank and we were dumped out into the ocean!! It was cold and dark! I went under the water and I couldn't come up. I couldn't get air! I couldn't breathe. I kicked and kicked, but I still couldn't come up. I was stuck under something. I couldn't yell for help. I didn't have any air left!

Laurence remembered that Mama had told him to "Watch out for Luella." He looked around and couldn't see me anywhere, but he saw a big man on top of something. He looked more closely, and this man was on top of arms and legs that were kicking and moving! They were mine! Laurence started to push and kick too, and he shoved as hard as he could! He kept pushing and shoving. He pushed that man off of me. I popped up! I came up to the top of the ocean. I was choking on water, but I was free! I could get air! I could breathe! My big brother saved me!

We all had our lifejackets on when we were dumped into the water, but when we came back up, Lois' lifejacket was missing. The water pulled it right off! It was good that Mama was holding her tight.

Mama looked and saw Wilfred. He was so little in his big lifejacket that he could hardly keep his head above the water. Mama reached as far as she could, pulled him close to her, and tried to fix his lifejacket so his head could be straight up. Eleanor and Evelyn were right next to each other. They looked like they were connected. We were all floating! Mama talked to us quietly when she could. She said to keep our mouths closed so we wouldn't choke on the salty water, but to pray in our hearts. The water stung my eyes. It was such a bad morning! I wanted someone to hold me!

It was very hard to float straight up. Every few minutes, Mama would call, "Luella." One time I didn't hear her and I didn't answer. She was afraid that I had drowned. But then I heard her voice, and I said, "Here I am, Mama."

Our lifeboat popped back up in the water, upside down. Some men helped Wilfred and Evelyn and me climb up on top of its bottom. We rocked and dipped with the waves, and I can't remember who got to be right in the middle. We sat as close together as we could. I tried to hold on because I didn't want to fall into the ocean again, but I couldn't stop shivering and shaking. My teeth were chattering. When I looked at Mama, she gave me a little smile. I knew I had to be brave and not cry, but most of all I wanted someone to hold me!

I didn't know Mama couldn't swim. She couldn't even swim an inch and was afraid of water, but she didn't tell us that. She just acted brave so that we would be brave too. She pretended to be swimming with an oar under one arm, her lifejacket tied around her, and little Lois in her other arm. Later she told us that she had someone helping her. She said, "God was swimming beside me all the time. That's what made me so strong."

I'm glad the sharks didn't come. Mama's foot was bleeding, and sharks like blood!

The sun said "good morning" to the world. So far it hadn't been good at all! What was going to happen to us? How long could we keep floating? Who could help us?

A big ship was coming toward us. It came closer and closer.

It wasn't the ZAMZAM. It was the ship that had tried to sink us, a German Raider! Maybe it was going to fire more shells at us. I was very scared, but something special happened. A big, perfect rainbow started shining in the sky with both ends touching the water. It was beautiful. Mama told us that it was a sign of God's promise that He would always take care of us. I looked at that rainbow in the sky and smiled a little smile. I think God was holding me!

What would this German Raider do to us? It didn't shoot at us. It didn't run into us, but it stopped near us and all the men on it looked and looked. They were surprised! They looked some more and shook their heads. They had attacked us because they thought the ZAMZAM had bombs and guns for fighting wars on it. Instead it had friendly people with only suitcases and sewing machines and toys. We were mamas and children. We wouldn't fight any war!

The Germans were sorry that they had tried to hurt us! It was a bad mistake. Now they wanted to rescue us and put us on their ship. So they pulled us out of the water, into an extra little boat; and took us to the side of their big German Raider.

The only way to get from the little boat up to the deck of the German Raider was by climbing up a rope ladder. It was a long ways to the top! Laurence was the first to look at the ladder and start to climb up it. He liked to climb tall trees and do scary things, so he knew he could do it. He was careful, though, and soon he went all the way from the little boat to the very top of the ladder and stepped onto the deck of the German Raider! Then it was time for Eleanor and Evelyn to do it. First Eleanor took her turn, and then Evelyn. They climbed and climbed and climbed, and the ladder kept swinging and swinging and swinging, and they did it! I watched and I did NOT want to climb up this ladder. I might get caught right in the middle and fall down into the middle of the ocean! It looked so scary and I was only four—really four-and-a-half. If Daddy were here, he could help me.

Mama looked right at me and touched my shoulders. She said, "Luella, it is your turn. You are brave and you can do it. Jesus will help you."

I held the ropes on the sides of the ladder very tight and I didn't look down at the dark water below me. I only looked up. The ladder kept swinging back and forth, back and forth. I lifted one leg and then the other, and I moved one hand and then the other up the ropes. I kept looking up, lifting each leg and moving each hand, and looking up, and the ladder kept swinging. But I did it!!!!! I climbed all the way to the top and stepped onto the deck. I was so proud! I didn't ever want to do it again!

Mama came up next, and she made it! Hurrah for Mama! Wilfred and Lois were too little to climb up like I did, so they each sat inside a basket pulled up by a rope tied to it. Oh, Mama was so happy when we all got up on the deck and she could stand right in the middle of all of us kids.

Everyone on the ZAMZAM was rescued! Not even one person drowned. Not even one person died. Not even one person was lost. The Captain of the German Raider could not believe this. He said it was a miracle. We were alive! We were all safe. It was a miracle!

Some people were hurt though, and Mama's foot kept bleeding. She had to limp. I felt sorry for her.

The ZAMZAM was still floating on the ocean, all tipped to one side with the big hole right in the middle and more holes around it. The Germans knew they had made an awful mistake when they fired the big shells at our boat. They didn't want anyone to know what they had done, so they needed to sink the ZAMZAM under the water. They would not tell anybody about this bad, bad morning.

Three time bombs were put on the ZAMZAM. These exploded
and our big ship sank down right into the middle of the ocean.
Every single bit of it sank to the bottom. Everything that
Mama had packed in the trunks and boxes sank. Laurence's
bike and his clarinet and his stamp collection sank! Our
dolls sank. The violin we were bringing to Daddy sank too.
Our clothes sank. All I had to wear was a little dress but no
underwear. I was very embarrassed. My big brother was even
more embarrassed. He had only a mattress cover to wear.
I didn't laugh at him, though, and he didn't laugh at me.
Nobody laughed at us. We were happy to be alive.

Now we were prisoners on the German Raider. We were
prisoners of war. We couldn't choose when to eat or where to
sleep or what to do or where to go. We had to do whatever
the Germans told us to do.

On the next day, the Captain of the German Raider switched

us to another ship named the Dresden. It was also a prison ship, but there was a little more room. However, we were still very crowded! All the men slept in one big room in the basement of the ship with no windows or lights or toilet. They used a bucket! It was very bad for them. A guard with a gun stood by the door when it was opened in the morning and closed at night. I'm glad I didn't have to sleep down there.

Mama, Laurence, Eleanor, Evelyn, Wilfred, Lois, one other lady, and I all stayed in one room. We only had two little beds so we took turns sleeping on the floor. It was good being close because it felt safer. We could say our bedtime prayers together, and we would sing our favorite song,
"Jesus, tender shepherd, hear me,
Bless your little lamb tonight.
Through the darkness be Thou near me,
Keep me safe 'til morning light."

The worst part about being on the prison ship was the food. We had soup and bread and then bread and soup—every day! The soup looked like dishwater and the bread was hard and sour and had bugs in it. I was so hungry I ate that buggy bread. One day I got part of a cookie. It was really two cookie crumbs stuck together with frosting right in the middle. I ate it and wished I could have one more, but there weren't any more. Another time we got an orange and we all shared it. Eleanor and Evelyn found some orange peelings on the deck. They picked them up and brought them to us for a treat. I was always hungry and my tummy hurt.

We had to be on the prison ship a long time, but the Germans were kind to us. They didn't yell or act mean. They tried to keep us safe. They told us to use our lifejackets for pillows in case we would be attacked by another warship in the middle of the night. That made it extra hard to go to sleep. I was afraid, but I knew that God never goes to sleep. He doesn't even take tiny naps. Thinking about that made me feel better. Besides, I thought about that special rainbow in the sky.

All of this time, no one knew where we were. Daddy in Africa didn't know where we were. Our friends back in Kansas didn't know where we were. Our grandpa and grandma didn't know where we were. Even the President of America didn't know where we were. No one knew that the ZAMZAM had been sunk. No one knew that we were prisoners. We had just disappeared. The Germans hadn't told anyone what they had done. They couldn't hide us forever, though. They were running out of food, so they needed to get to land!

Daddy was very worried. He hadn't heard from us for a long time and we were supposed to be in Africa. Instead we were on the prison ship, and he didn't know that.

Then Daddy heard some awful news on the radio in Africa. He heard the ZAMZAM was lost! He thought we were all gone. He cried and cried and could not stop! Two days later, he heard some good news. The passengers on the ZAMZAM had come to land. Maybe we were alive! Maybe he could see us! It was his birthday, and he felt God had given him a great big birthday present wrapped up in a rainbow!!!

The land we came to was France. The Germans said we could be free if we were Americans, but if we were from some other countries, we would have to go to a prison camp. Everyone in our family was an American so we were happy, but we were sad for some of our friends who couldn't be free. I cried when I heard that Peter and Wendy had to go to a prison camp. They were my friends, just my size, and their mother's leg had been hurt real bad. They were not Americans, and they were taken to be prisoners again.

It was good to be on real land and touch the dirt. We played hopscotch. Then all kinds of good things started to happen. Someone gave me some white bread and I put butter and sugar on it. Each of us got a real bed to sleep in. The Red Cross looked in their boxes and found clothes for us to wear. I got a little shirt with red stripes on it. I tried to be all happy, but inside I was still sad and frightened. All the noisy explosions and our lifeboat sinking and climbing up that rope ladder and the awful food and thinking we would be attacked again and again had left bad memories in my heart. The only thing that made me feel better was remembering the rainbow in the sky.

After many days on land, our family heard we could go back to America. Reporters started taking lots of pictures of us.

We got on a ship and came to New York and people acted like we were famous. Our pictures were right in the middle of the front page of all of the newspapers. Everyone wanted to talk to Mama and hear the ZAMZAM story. They said how brave Mama was, but do you know what she said? She said it was God who really saved us and that's what we should tell others. So I wanted to tell you the story of the ZAMZAM.

LILLIAN DANIELSON *and her children, in a 1941 photo, arrive in New York more than two months after the sinking of the Zamzam. The children are Eleanor, Laurence, Wilfred, Luella, Lois and Evelyn.*

My story is not over, though, until I tell you the very ending. Mama and all of us kids came back to Kansas to our special house with the five big closets right in the middle of our little town, in the middle of Kansas, right in the middle of America. We waited and waited for our Daddy to come home. For more than three more years we waited, and then it happened. We heard that Daddy was coming. He was coming home! I was excited, but I also was worried because I hadn't seen him for such a long time. Maybe he wouldn't know who I was. When he left, I was only three years old, and now I was eight. And what about Baby Lois? Would he know her? She wasn't a baby anymore, but a five-year-old girl! And what about Laurence? He had grown so much that Mama said he was taller than Daddy.

What would Daddy be like? Would he know how to do "Daddy things" like play ball and swing me and fly a kite? Would he like to eat cupcakes with frosting on the top, or maybe right in the middle? Would he want to hold me?

Well.....our Daddy came home! He came on the train, and we all went to meet him. Mama wore a beautiful black hat so she would look lovely. She made pretty curls in my sisters' and my hair. Laurence put on a suit and Wilfred dressed up in a white shirt. We looked very fancy!

We stood at the train depot when the noisy train came rumbling in and stopped. The door opened, and then..... right there in the middle was Daddy standing in his big brown overcoat and his gentleman's hat. He stepped off the train, looked at Mama and put his arms around her and hugged and kissed her while we watched. He looked at each one of us— six grown-up children who had waited and waited for him to come home. He hugged and kissed us and held me tight. I was so happy to be right in the middle of his arms!

We all got into a car. I held his hand and saw tears in his eyes. One rolled right down his cheek and he didn't even wipe it away. He just let it fall onto his coat as he kept smiling. I loved him so much, and now we were a happy family all together.

One hour after being reunited,
we stand outside our home in Lindsborg, Kansas.
November 5, 1944

This is my true story, and I always smile when I see a rainbow in the sky. And I have decided that I really like "Faith" and I'm going to keep it right in the middle of my name!

Luella Faith

Printed in the United States
by Baker & Taylor Publisher Services